OUR LIVING PLANET

Rain Forests

BLACKBIRCH®
PRESS

THOMSON
GALE

San Diego • Detroit • New York • San Francisco • Cleveland
New Haven, Conn. • Waterville, Maine • London • Munich

THOMSON
GALE

For more information, contact
The Gale Group, Inc.
27500 Drake Rd.
Farmington Hills, MI 48331-3535
Or you can visit our Internet site at http://www.gale.com

Adapted by A S Publishing from
Las Selvas © Parramon Ediciones S.A. 1996

Editor: Rosa Fragua
Text: Marta Serrano
Illustrations: Marcel Socias
Design: Beatriz Seoane
Layout: Josep Guasch
Production: Rafael Marfil

LIBRARY OF CONGRESS CATALOGING-IN-PUBLICATION DATA

Serrano, Marta.
 Rain forests / by Marta Serrano.
  p. cm. — (Living planet series)
Summary: Discusses the weather, life forms, soil, animals, and ecology of rain forests.
 ISBN 1-56711-670-1
 1. Rain forest ecology—Juvenile literature. [1. Rain forests. 2. Rain forest ecology. 3. Ecology.]
I. Title. II. Series.
 QH541.5.R27 S47 2003
 577.34—dc21   2002009532

Printed in Spain
10 9 8 7 6 5 4 3 2 1

CONTENTS

INSIDE THE RAIN FORESTS

Tropical rain forests grow in warm areas of the world that have plenty of rainfall. They are home to a greater variety of living things than any other habitat on earth. Among the t all trees live millions of plants, animals, and microscopic organisms. Some of the world's most colorful creatures, including parrots (right), live among the dark green trees.

From above, rain forests look like enormous green rugs. An aerial view reveals only one of several layers—the canopy, which is made up of the tops of tall trees. The canopy is from 82 to 148 feet (25 to 45 m) high. Trees called emergents are even taller, and rise above the canopy to heights of 197 to 230 feet (60 to 70 m). Beneath the canopy, at about 49.2 feet (15 m), smaller trees and shrubs form an understory. Palms are the most common trees in the understory.

In the rain forests, scientists find plants and animals that have not yet been named or studied. Large areas of the forests have never even been mapped.

The crowns of the trees prevent most of the sunlight from reaching the forest floor—the forest's lowest level. In the humid darkness under the trees, fungi and bacteria help to break down the leaves and other plant materials that fall to the ground.

The canopy protects the lower levels of the forest from the impact of heavy rain and strong winds that would otherwise wash away the soil. The trees also support many smaller plants. Epiphytes—such as orchids, bromeliads, and ferns—perch high in the branches. They get their moisture from the damp air and their minerals from animal droppings and dead leaves. Woody vines, called lianas, twist around trunks and emerge at the tops of the trees. Many of the plants produce bright flowers and luscious fruits.

Plants cannot grow without sunlight. The emergents and the trees in the canopy are bathed in sunlight every day, but other plants must climb or perch to receive light. Only when a tall tree falls does light reach the forest floor. Then, seeds that fall to the ground put out roots and shoots that will later grow toward the light.

The only parts of the forest where plants, at all levels, benefit from the sun are the banks of the many rivers that wind through the trees. Dense tangles of undergrowth exist by the water's edge. Many types of fish live in the muddy waters. They are an important source of food for the people who live near the forest.

The rain forest may look empty, but it is rarely quiet. Rain thunders or drips, while branches and leaves rustle. Birds screech and twitter in the trees, monkeys chatter, frogs croak, and insects buzz and whine.

The people of the rain forest are skilled in finding food and conserving the plants and animals that newcomers often destroy.

AN ABUNDANCE OF LIFE

Tropical rain forests cover only about 7 percent of the earth's land surface. Despite their small land area, they contain more than half of all the world's known species of living plants and animals. An area the size of a football field contains an average of 300 species of trees. One of those trees alone may support as many as 150 kinds of beetles. Scientists think there are still more organisms to be discovered.

The great diversity of life in rain forests is due to the forests' location near the equator, where the hot and generally wet climate favors plant growth.

The variety of life in an area is known as its biodiversity. The richness of the rain forest's bio-diversity probably results from its inaccessibility and climate. The hot and rainy conditions of lands near the equator encouraged the lush growth of plants, which then encouraged the evolution of many animals. Because rain forests have a low population of people, their evolution has been relatively undisturbed, at least until recent times.

The plants and animals have many special adaptations. The hummingbird (above) has a beak that is specially adapted to feed from deep-throated tubular flowers. Bees and other insects cannot steal the nectar because they cannot reach far enough into the flower. The toucan (left) eats mostly small fruits, with its enormous but lightweight

beak. The serrated edge helps it to carve chunks off larger pieces of fruit.

Some rain forests have a greater biodiversity than others. These areas are known as hot spots. They contain a quarter of all the tropical forest plant species. Scientists believe that these rich areas should be preserved for the sake of future generations.

Rain forests contain many of the world's tallest trees and most beautiful flowers, such as orchids, which are one of the world's largest plant families. Many orchids grow on the trunks and branches of trees, alongside the twisting, twining lianas (left) that festoon the tree trunks. Some orchids have a special relationship with certain animals. For example, only one kind of hummingbird can feed from one kind of orchid.

More than 80 percent of the world's insects live in the forests. Butterflies are among the most colorful. They thrive because there is so much nectar for them to drink. Their caterpillars, in turn, provide food for the birds.

Rain forests contain so many plant species that there is a continuous supply of flowers, fruits, and seeds for the forest animals. Plants also provide shelter for the animals.

Creatures in the rain forests get nourishment in many ways. Some butterflies suck nectar from flowers; others feed on animal droppings.

FOREST VEGETATION

The sun's heat is strongest in regions around the equator and weakest at the north and south poles. As a result, the tropics (the lands around the equator) are the hottest places on earth, while polar regions are the coldest.

In lowlands near the equator, temperatures rarely fall below 68°F (20°C) throughout the year. In addition, these areas get plenty of rain, which encourages the thick and fast growth of rainforest plants all year long. In many areas, rain falls every day, so there are no seasons. Temperatures drop as height increases, so mist (below) and even snow occur on highlands in the tropics.

Solar radiation is greatest in places near the equator. In places far away from the equator, the sun's rays are spread over much larger areas, so they are much cooler. Rain forests grow only in hot, wet regions.

Highland rain forest

Lowland rain forest

Mangrove swamp

Sea

The intense heat of the sun in the tropics causes the water in the oceans, lakes, and rivers to evaporate. The water turns to vapor and makes the air humid. Plants also give off water, in a process called transpiration, and add more moisture to the vapor in the air. The hot, humid air rises and cools. As it cools, the invisible water vapor in the air condenses into visible droplets of water to form clouds. The clouds grow until the droplets merge into raindrops that fall to the ground, often in thunderous downpours of immense force.

Transpiration from the rainforest plants is responsible for almost half the rain that falls on the forests. In mountainous parts of the tropics, temperatures are lower than they are in the lowlands. Vegetation is less dense, so there is less transpiration and less rain, whereas on the high slopes, there are constant clouds.

The plants and animals vary with altitude. In the lowlands, where rivers flow, larger animals like the rare Javan rhinoceros (below) find a home. Higher up, the animals and plants are smaller.

In some rain forests, thunderstorms occur almost daily, usually in the late afternoon. The average yearly rainfall ranges from 97.5 inches (2,500 mm) to more than 234 inches (6,000 mm).

RAIN FORESTS OF THE WORLD

The world's rainforest regions are mostly in the tropics. There are no natural rain forests in Europe.

The world's largest rain forest is in South America, in the Amazon River Basin. It stretches across the continent from Peru in the west through Brazil to the Atlantic Coast in the east. It covers about 2 million square miles (5.2 million sq km). In central Africa, the second largest region of rain forest covers the basin of the Congo River. Other rain forests grow on the island of Madagascar, in southern and southeastern Asia, southern China, northern Australia, New Guinea, and on some Pacific islands.

There are three main types of rain forest: lowland, cloud, and monsoon. Lowland rain forests have rain throughout the year, so the trees grow very tall. These rain forests occur mostly in areas that are drained by large rivers.

Cloud forests (top) occur in highland areas and are often bathed in mist. In them, trees are shorter than those in lowland rain forests and less crowded together.

Monsoon forests occur in tropical regions where there are both wet and dry seasons. These forests occur mostly in Asia, such as in Indonesia and Malaysia, where orangutans (left) are found. Lowland rain forests and cloud forests are always green. In monsoon forests, some of the trees shed their leaves in the dry season.

The Amazon River (right) winds its sluggish way

through the rain forest. Hundreds of smaller tributaries run into it.

From the air, all rain forests look similar, even though they are not. The various rain forests contain different species of plants and animals, and different species live in separate parts of the same forest. Many of the trees that grow in highland areas, for example, do not grow in lowland areas.

Australia and New Guinea's rain forests are home to creatures that live nowhere else on earth. Many of them are marsupials, like the cuscus (above). Its big eyes help it to see well in the darkness of the trees.

Despite the great distances between the rain forests of South America, Africa, and Asia, many of the plants and animals are similar, because they have evolved under similar conditions. Monkeys, for example, live in all of these rain forests.

Mangrove trees grow in swampy water along tropical seacoasts. They send down roots that grow into supporting "stilts."

FOREST SOILS

Although rain forests boast the most abundant plant life on earth, the soil is mostly infertile. The growing plants quickly use up the nutrients in the soil. When trees are cut down, heavy rains quickly wash the nutrients from the top layers of the soil, which makes the soil useless for growing plants.

The nutrients that plants need for growth come from organic matter—plants and animals that have died and decayed. Dead leaves, fallen branches, dead animals, and animal droppings are full of nutrients. These substances decay rapidly on the hot, humid forest floor. Fungi and bacteria encourage decay and turn the dead matter into minerals that can be absorbed by the roots of plants. Some creatures, such as centipedes (below), live on the forest floor.

Because the nutrients lie on or near the surface, most trees have shallow roots. Shallow roots cannot support tall, heavy trees, and so many trees produce a second means of support. These are huge buttress roots (above) that grow up to 16.4 feet (5 m) high above the ground. The buttresses increase the thickness of the trunk and give support to the trees.

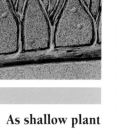

As shallow plant roots spread through the soil, the roots extract nutrients as soon as they become available through the process of decay.

In many rain forests, the ground is covered by a spongy mass of tangled roots, fungi (right), humus (rotted material), bacteria, and other microorganisms. The roots of plants gain nutrients from this spongy layer.

Many of the shallow tree roots are invaded by mycorrhizae. These are the minute underground threads of numerous types of fungi. The hairlike threads absorb water and minerals from the humus and supply it to the tree's root. Many trees absorb most of the substances they need through the mycorrhizae and could not live without them. Bracket fungi (right) live on the branches of both dead and living trees. They take nourishment from the tree, but do not necessarily kill it.

The plants take up the nutrients from the decaying matter on the forest floor, before the nutrients have a chance to sink into the soil's depths. The rapid decay and reuse of nutrients works well, as long as the plants are undisturbed. If the trees are cut down, the supply of decayed material is reduced. Forest clearance allows rainwater to wash away the nutrients in the soil. The mycorrhizae—and many other vital organisms—then begin to disappear, and the ground gradually becomes infertile.

The roots of the trees do not dig deep into the ground. Instead, they spread out around the trees to reach more nutrients and to brace the trunks.

RIVERS AND FLOODS

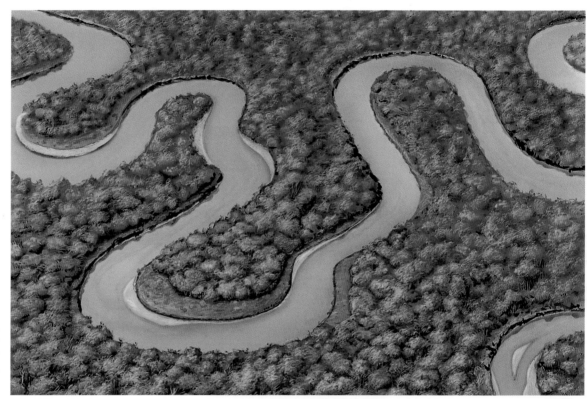

The notorious piranha fish lives in the Amazon. Schools of these sharp-toothed fish may attack and devour larger animals that stray into the water.

The Amazon River in South America (above) is the world's largest river. It is wide and deep, and in places stretches 6.2 miles (10 km) from bank to bank. The Nile in Africa is longer, but because of the abundant rainfall the Amazon receives, it contains more water than the Nile, the Mississippi, and the Chang (or Yangtze) in China put together. The Congo in Africa is the world's second largest river. It, too, is fed by abundant rainfall.

The river is the main highway of the rain forest. It is home to many types of fish and other creatures. The Amazon dolphin (right) is a freshwater mammal that lives up to 1,860 miles (3,000 km) from the sea.

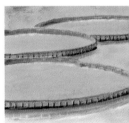

Many dangerous animals live along the banks of rainforest rivers, such as alligators, crocodiles, and caimans. These creatures lurk in the water, ready to snap up their prey in their huge jaws. Their lashing tails help them to move swiftly in the water and on land.

The anaconda (above) is one of the world's largest snakes and can grow up to 29.5 feet (9 m) long. It is immensely powerful and swims well underwater. The anaconda seizes a victim, squeezes the life out of it, and then brings it ashore to devour. Anacondas also catch small birds, mammals, and reptiles on the riverbank and have even been known to attack and kill small caimans.

Periodically, when extra-heavy rains fall in the mountains, tropical rivers become swollen with water and overflow their banks downstream. This causes great floods. Floods occur in all rain forests. They turn large areas into shallow lakes, with wooded islands (top) and waterways (right) that run between strips of high ground like canals.

Rainforest plants have adapted to survive this annual drowning. Their roots can withstand the lack of oxygen. When the floods recede, they benefit from the silt that is dumped over the land by the river water. This fertile silt contains minerals that the plants need.

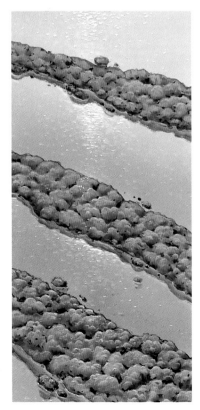

Giant water lilies are common in the Amazon. Their floating leaves have upturned rims and can support the weight of a baby. They provide shelter for many small water creatures.

15

COMPETING FOR LIGHT

Because of the lack of sunlight, the plant life in the bottom layer of the rain forest is less abundant than it is higher up. Although some shrubs and bushes grow in the depths of the forest, the ground is mostly bare. There is not even a layer of dead leaves, because the warm, damp atmosphere ensures that the leaves decay almost as soon as they fall.

There is some stunted growth of germinated seeds, but their pale shoots fail to grow in the gloomy conditions. Other seeds lie dormant while they wait for enough light to germinate. The situation changes when a tree dies and collapses (above).

Trees may die of old age or because they have been eaten away by parasites. Others are blown down by strong winds. When a tree crashes to the ground, it often takes some branches of other nearby trees with it.

This creates a gap in the dense canopy, which results in an immediate burst of growth (below). Seeds germinate in the clearing. Saplings race toward the light, while creepers scramble after them.

When a falling tree creates a gap in the forest, plants grow quickly and create dense undergrowth that is hard to penetrate. Such undergrowth grows along riverbanks.

When a tree falls (right), it does not take long before the vigorous growth of plants closes the gap and restores the canopy. Not all clearings are natural. Some are created by rainforest people who "slash and burn" the trees to create small plots for farming. At first, food plants grow well, but soon the nutrients are used up or washed away by heavy rain. The people then move on to a new plot and allow the forest to grow again.

Much rain forest is cut down for timber or burned (below) to clear land for agriculture. When the land is later abandoned, the forest may grow back, but with fewer species of trees and more undergrowth.

In 1997, vast areas of forest in Indonesia blazed for weeks. The smoke caused choking fogs in distant cities. The fires had been started deliberately to clear land for agriculture.

FOREST ANIMALS

Until recently, conditions in the rain forests had remained nearly the same for thousands of years. As a result, many plants and animals have developed relationships with each other that are so close that they cannot survive apart. Plants provide food and shelter for animals. In return, the animals help to pollinate plants and spread their seeds. Some animals eat only other animals, some eat only plants, and others eat both.

An amazing relationship exists between leaf-cutter ants and the plant world (top). Leaf-cutters bite off pieces of leaves and carry them back to their nests. There, they chew the leaves and plant them in a "garden," where they grow a special type of fungus. This fungus, which provides food for the ants, is found only in the nests of leaf-cutter ants.

Tent-making bats (right) spend the daytime hiding under large leaves. They often cut through the leaf veins, so that the stiff leaves collapse around them to form an even cozier shelter.

The plants in rain forests provide food for herbivores, or plant eaters. In turn, the herbivores provide food for the carnivores, or meat eaters, like this jaguar.

Many plant-eating animals are highly specialized and feed only on certain fruits. Others feed only on leaves, seeds, nectar, pollen, or rotting plant remains. Plant-eating animals in the rain forests range from massive Indian elephants (above) to tiny insects.

Herbivores and other carnivores provide food for predators, such as crocodiles, leopards, spiders, and snakes, as well as many birds and insects. The gavial, a type of crocodile that lives in Asia (below), snaps up fish with a sideways swipe of its long jaws. It lays many eggs, but not many baby gavials escape the jaws of riverbank predators.

Other smaller predators include the insectivores that feed only on insects. Scavengers, which live on dead animals, are not common in rain forests, because flesh decays quickly in the hot and humid conditions.

Huge numbers of insect-eating bats flit through the forest at night. They use echoes to locate their prey in the dark. Some of the larger bats feed on fruit and are called flying foxes.

LIFE IN THE TREES

There is food in the treetops all year long. Animals that can fly, such as birds, bats, and many insects, can reach it easily. Most of the birds have short, rounded wings that make it easier for them to fly through narrow spaces. Animals that cannot fly must either climb or leap. Some have developed special adaptations to help them scramble through the trees and hold onto branches. These features include prehensile hands and feet that can grasp like human hands.

Some monkeys, like the spider monkey of Central and South America (right), also have prehensile tails. Chimpanzees (below) are apes that live in Africa. They have no tails, but they can move easily through the branches or over the ground.

Some rainforest species have adapted to life in the trees by developing the ability to glide from branch to branch.

Reptiles and amphibians cannot fly in the way that birds can, but many rainforest species have developed the ability to glide or parachute and to cling to surfaces when they are upside down or caught in a strong wind or downpour. Suction pads or hairs on their feet help them to grip even smooth surfaces. Webbed feet and flaps of skin can be spread for gliding or stopping a fall. The gecko (above) has webbed feet and a fringe of skin all around its body that enables it to glide for several feet.

Bats are the only mammals that can truly fly. Flying squirrels glide. The squirrel (right) has folds of skin between its arms and legs. With these held taut by its outstretched limbs, it launches its lightweight body into the air and lands gracefully several feet away. Some flying squirrels have been known to cover distances of over 164 feet (50 m) in one leap.

A flying frog extends its webbed feet to parachute from one branch to another. It can glide 16.4 feet (5 m) in one leap.

21

POISONS AND MEDICINES

Many rainforest plants contain poisons that prevent them from being eaten and keep them safe from attack by bacteria and viruses that cause disease. The people of the rain forests know about these substances and use them in their daily life. They grind the seeds of guarana fruits (right) to make a strong drink that is similar to coffee. Poisonous hairs protect the bird-eating spider (below).

The hunters of the South American rainforests tip their arrows with deadly poison from a tiny frog.

The rainforest people have a wide knowledge of the plants that can be used as medicines. Curare is a poisonous substance used by hunters in the Amazon Basin to tip their arrows. It comes from the bark of a liana. The poison paralyzes the victim's muscles. Doctors throughout the world also use curare, but as a drug to help relax muscles when people undergo surgery. Many other drugs and medicines are derived from rainforest plants and animals. Scientists hope to find new ones that may help to cure diseases for which no cures are yet known.

Many rainforest snakes use venom to paralyze or kill their prey. Some, like this African gaboon viper (above), are well camouflaged and hard to see on the forest floor, as they wait for their prey.

The arrow-poison frog (below) advertises its presence with its bright red skin. The color warns predators that it is poisonous. This helps to protect the frog from other animals, but not from humans. Hunters, who use the frog's poison to tip their arrows, have little difficulty in spotting the tiny creatures against the dark green foliage.

The fruit of the guarana looks like a winking eye. People make a drink from it that helps to remove parasites from the intestines.

FOREST PRODUCTS

Rain forests contain important resources that can be used not only by the local people but also by people throughout the world. More than one fourth of the world's medicines contain ingredients that come from rainforest plants. Unfortunately, rain forests are now being destroyed before anyone has a chance to study valuable species. Large areas have been cleared to grow crops on plantations.

Many medicines come from rainforest plants. The discovery of new species may enable scientists to develop life-saving drugs.

1. Mango
2. Papaya
3. Brazil nut
4. Tamarind
5. Zebrawood fruit
6. Nutmeg
7. Cherimoya
8. Pupunha

1

2

3

5

6

7

The most valuable of all timber comes from the rain forests. Slow-growing trees produce the finest hardwoods. Coniferous trees grow fast, but their wood is mostly softwood. The most highly prized woods include brazilwood, ebony, mahogany, rosewood, and teak. Some of the trees that have taken more than a thousand years to grow are felled in minutes (top).

Many fruits and nuts can be harvested in small quantities from the trees. Others are grown on plantations in forest clearings or elsewhere. Cocoa (center right), coffee, and vanilla are all rainforest species. Natural rubber is made from the latex that flows from rubber trees (bottom right).

Once, there were many rubber plantations in Brazil, where rubber trees originally came from. Now most natural rubber is produced in Southeast Asia.

4

8

DISAPPEARING FORESTS

The building of roads not only scars the forest but also encourages settlers who destroy even more forest.

Forest that remains undisturbed is called virgin forest or primary forest. Areas that have regrown (left) are called secondary forest. They have fewer slow-growing trees and more undergrowth. A few thousand years ago, virgin rain forest covered about 14 percent of the earth's land surface. Today, half of that area has already gone. Some experts estimate that a rainforest area the size of 25 football fields disappears every minute. At that rate, the Amazon Rain Forest will disappear in 200 years.

In the past, when only a few small groups of people lived in the forest, they did little harm. They knew how to grow or find food and to obtain the necessities of life without damaging the forest. Increasing numbers of people now live in and near the forests. They mostly do not respect the forest in the same way and seek to exploit its resources.

Logging (left) is a major cause of deforestation. Loggers often want only the most valuable tree species, but they must cut down other trees to reach them. Forest is also cleared for mines (top right), and the trees are then used as fuel for smelting. Dams are constructed to provide hydro-electricity. Roads and pipelines are built to convey the oil, gold, iron ore, and other minerals that are extracted.

Rain forest is also turned into grazing land for beef cattle. Local people clear the land, initially to grow crops. Often, they burn down the trees. After a few years, their crops fail because the soil is exhausted. Cattle farmers then buy the land and turn it into pasture, right. But the pasture lasts for only about ten years. Then, the land is useless, and the areas are too large for the forest to regrow. What soil remains is blown or washed away, which leaves behind exposed rock.

The loss of the rain forests is a global problem. The local people, like the women in the picture (below), are poor and desperate to make a living. They cannot be blamed for their attempts to feed their families. Other countries are more to blame, because their citizens want rainforest products. More people now realize how much will be lost if the forests disappear, and are making efforts to conserve them.

Spraying poor soil with fertilizers and crops with pesticides does the land more harm than good.

UNDERSTANDING RAIN FORESTS

HOW PLANTS "SWEAT"

The air in rain forests is extremely humid. Plant transpiration causes high humidity. To see transpiration occur, place a plastic bag over the leaves of a plant and put it in the sun. Before long, you will see that droplets of water have formed on the inside of the bag. This is because the plant gives off water vapor through its leaves. This water vapor condenses into water droplets on the plastic surface. Imagine how much water all the plants in a rain forest give off.

IMITATING A RAINFOREST

Even in the middle of the day, when the sun is high in the sky, it is always quite dark at ground level in the rain forest. This is because the dense layers of leaves in the canopy and understory of the forest do not allow much sunlight to filter down to ground level. The gloomy conditions on the ground in a rain forest prevent the normal development of plants.

It is easy to see what happens when plants do not get enough light. Take a seed box and grow one type of plant in it. When the seedlings appear, place a sheet of black plastic container liner over half of the box. Use sticks to prop up the plastic to ensure that it does not touch the plants. Over the next few days, lift the plastic only when you need to water the plants. Give an equal amount of water to both sides. After some time, you will see that the uncovered plants grow well, while the covered plants are weak and spindly. This shows that plants need plenty of sunlight, as well as soil and water.

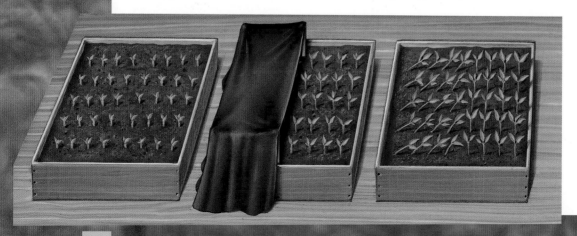

WEATHER CONTROL

Around the equator, where most of the world's rain forests are found, weather conditions remain much the same throughout the year. These constant conditions of great heat and abundant rainfall are highly favorable for plant growth. To the north and south of the tropics lie regions with distinct seasons. Seasons have a great effect on plants. This is because plant growth slows down, or even stops, during periods of intense heat or cold.

Greenhouses are used to produce plants that need constant heat and humidity. Gardeners can grow tropical fruits in greenhouses. They also grow local fruits out of season. They can do this because weather conditions can be controlled. Greenhouse plants can enjoy continuous warmth and plenty of moisture.

FOOD FOR FUNGI

Dead organic matter, whether plant or animal, decomposes (rots) very quickly in rain forests. This is because the conditions are perfect for the organisms responsible for decomposition. The best known of these organisms are fungi. The familiar mushroom is an edible fungus. The mold that grows on food that is no longer fresh is also a fungus.

If you want to see molds grow, choose a food they like. Leave a tomato or some stale bread in the open. Keep it damp, then watch the patches of mold appear. See whether a tomato in the refrigerator develops mold as quickly.

It is always best to throw away food that has turned moldy. Be sure to keep it away from other food, because molds can spread very quickly.

GLOSSARY

ADAPTATION Changes in the body or behavior of an animal or plant that help it to survive in its environment.

AMPHIBIANS A group of animals that includes frogs, toads, newts, and salamanders. Most of them spend part of their lives in water and part on land.

BACTERIA Microorganisms that exist everywhere in nature. Some are harmful, some beneficial.

BASIN An area drained by a river and its tributaries.

BIODIVERSITY The variety of species found in any natural region.

BOA Any of several large South American snakes that kill their prey by squeezing, or constricting, them.

BROMELIADS A group of tropical plants, including the pineapple, with rosettes of stiff leaves. Many are epiphytes.

BUTTRESS ROOTS Large roots that support many tall tropical trees—they act like the stone buttresses on a cathedral.

CAMOUFLAGE Coloring or pattern of skin that allows an animal to blend in with its background.

CANOPY The dense, leafy layer formed by the tops of trees in rain forests.

CARNIVORE An animal that eats meat rather than plants.

CLIMATE The usual or average weather at any place on earth.

CLOUD FOREST Areas of forest that are so high up that they are almost permanently shrouded in mist.

CONDENSE/CONDENSATION The change of state from a gas or vapor into a liquid.

DEBRIS Material formed from dead plants or worn rocks.

DEFORESTATION The cutting down and removal of trees.

DORMANT Asleep, or in a state of suspended animation.

EMERGENTS The tallest trees and the plants that reach the sunlight by living on or scrambling up to the top of the trees.

EPIPHYTES Plants that grow on other plants or surfaces, but get their moisture and nourishment from the air, not from the plant.

EQUATOR An imaginary line around the earth, exactly halfway between the north and south poles.

EVAPORATE/EVAPORATION The change that occurs when a liquid becomes a vapor, or gas.

EVOLUTION The gradual development of living things from simple organisms to complex ones.

EVOLVE To change over successive generations.

FUNGI Organisms, including mushrooms and molds, that absorb their food from living and dead organic matter.

GERMINATE To begin to grow. A seed germinates by putting down a root and sending up a shoot.

HABITAT A place where certain plants or animals normally live. herbivore An animal that feeds on plants.

HOT SPOTS A small number of places that are particularly rich in biodiversity.

HUMID Describes moist or damp conditions.

HUMIDITY The amount of water vapor in the air.

HUMUS Important part of the soil that is formed from decayed living matter.

HYDROELECTRICITY Electricity generated by the power of water being forced through a dam and spinning turbines.

INSECTIVORE An animal, such as an anteater, that lives on insects. intestines Part of the digestive system.

LATEX A milky substance produced by some plants, including rubber trees.

LIANA Any kind of woody creeping vine or plant that climbs up trees.

MANGROVE A type of tree with stilt roots that lives on coasts.

MICROORGANISM Any organism that is too small to be seen without a microscope; many are single-celled.

MONSOON A seasonal wind.

MYCORRHIZAE Fungus "threads" that live in tree roots and supply them with food.

NUTRIENT Food or any other substance, including minerals, that provides nourishment for plants or animals.

ORCHIDS A large family of flowering plants, many of which are epiphytes.

ORGANISM A living thing.

PALMS Woody plants, including dates, oil palms, and coconuts, with tall trunks and large leaves.

PARASITE An organism that feeds on another living organism (called a host).

PLANTATION Large farm planted with a single crop such as cocoa or rubber.

POLAR REGIONS The cold regions around the north and south poles.

POLES Two points (north and south) that mark the ends of the earth's axis, the imaginary line around which the earth rotates.

POLLINATION The transfer of pollen from the male part of a plant to the female part of the same or another plant, which enables it to produce seeds.

PREDATOR An animal that catches and eats other animals.

PREHENSILE The ability of hands, feet, and the tails of some animals to grasp.

REPTILES A group of cold-blooded animals that includes crocodiles, lizards, snakes, and turtles.

RODENTS A group of mammals, including beavers and squirrels, whose teeth are adapted to gnawing through hard objects.

SAPLING A young tree.

SCAVENGERS Animals that eat the bodies of dead animals.

SECONDARY FOREST Rain forest that has regrown, usually with fewer species, after being logged.

SILT Fine material worn from rocks that is found in lakes and rivers.

SLASH AND BURN A type of farming where farmers cut down and burn the natural vegetation to clear a plot for growing crops. When crop yields fall, the farmers clear a new plot.

SOLAR RADIATION The energy that comes from the sun.

SPECIES The basic unit of scientific classification of animals and plants. Members of a species can breed together.

STILT ROOTS Roots that lift a tree and its branches clear of floods and standing water.

TRANSPIRATION The giving off of water by the leaves of a plant.

TRIBUTARIES Rivers that flow into a main river.

TROPICAL From or to do with the tropics.

TROPICS The region between the tropic of Cancer and the tropic of Capricorn, two imaginary lines north and south of the equator. It is the world's hottest zone.

UNDERGROWTH The tangle of shrubs and bushes that grows under trees in exposed parts of a forest.

UNDERSTORY The layer of trees that grows under the canopy.

VEGETATION Growing plants.

VIRGIN FOREST Forests that have remained undisturbed since they first grew long ago.

VIRUS Disease-causing microorganism that can grow and multiply only inside the cells of plants and animals.

WATER VAPOR An invisible form of water that behaves like a gas.

INDEX